THE BARREN BRINGING FORTH

BRENDALEE BONNIE

THE BARREN BRINGING FORTH. Copyright @ 2024. Brendalee Bonnie. All rights reserved.

No part of this publication may be reproduced, stored in a retrieval system or transmitted in any form or by any means, electronic, mechanical, photocopying, recording or otherwise without the prior written permission of the author.

Published by:

Editor: Cleveland O. McLeish (Author C. Orville McLeish)

ISBN: 978-1-965635-04-9 (Paperback)

Scripture quotations marked (NIV) are taken from the Holy Bible, New International Version®, NIV®. Copyright © 1973, 1978, 1984 by Biblica, Inc.™ Used by permission of Zondervan. All rights reserved worldwide.

Scripture quotations marked "NKJV" are taken from the New King James Version. Copyright © 1982 by Thomas Nelson, Inc. Used by permission. All rights reserved. Bible text from the New King James Version® is not to be reproduced in copies or otherwise by any means except as permitted in writing by Thomas Nelson, Inc., Attn: Bible Rights and Permissions, P.O. Box 141000, Nashville, TN 37214-1000.

> "Sing, O barren,
> You who have not borne!
> Break forth into singing, and cry aloud,
> You who have not labored with child!
> For more are the children of the desolate
> Than the children of the married woman," says the LORD.
> "Enlarge the place of your tent,
> And let them stretch out the curtains of your dwellings;
> Do not spare;
> Lengthen your cords,
> And strengthen your stakes.
> For you shall expand to the right and to the left,
> And your descendants will inherit the nations,
> And make the desolate cities inhabited."
> (Isaiah 54:1-3 - NKJV).

TABLE OF CONTENTS

Introduction 7
Chapter 1: Understanding Barrenness 9
Chapter 2: Sarah 17
Chapter 3: Rebekah 23
Chapter 4: Rachel 27
Chapter 5: Hannah 31
Chapter 6: Overcoming Barrenness 39
The Declaratory Prayer of Faith 53
My Notes 55
Aspiring to Inspire 57
The Journey to Destiny Series 61

INTRODUCTION

This book was birthed in my spirit on September 13, 2023, while preparing my daily devotional, "The Birthing of the Barren."

As I studied carefully the stories of Hannah and Sarah, I heard "A book on the barren focusing on barren women;" then I heard the name released in my spirit, "The Barren Bringing Forth."

In this book, we will be looking at the journey of some barren women who gave birth to purpose and destiny as God removed their reproach and humiliated the adversary. Yes, indeed, their physical children had God's purpose or assignment locked inside them.

This book intends to highlight the journey of the barren and their stories, which declare God's glory. It will highlight God's majestic, transforming power, which is able to turn nothing into something and make the empty produce plenty and the barren not just produce good or more fruit but much fruit.

It will remind us and give evidence that there is nothing too hard or impossible for God because His grace is more than sufficient.

> "Is anything too hard for the LORD? At the appointed time I will return to you, according to the time of life, and Sarah shall have a son." (Genesis 18:14 - NKJV).

'Ah, Lord GOD! Behold, You have made the heavens and the earth by Your great power and outstretched arm. There is nothing too hard for You.' (Jeremiah 32:17 - NKJV).

For with God nothing will be impossible. (Luke 1:37 - NKJV).

CHAPTER 1: UNDERSTANDING BARRENNESS

Barrenness means infertility, unfruitfulness, emptiness, being closed-up, hopeless, helpless, and a state of being unproductive. It could be in the area of childbearing or in other areas of life; it could be either spiritual or physical barrenness. For example, when someone cannot conceive a child, it is a sign of barrenness. Another example is when a man cannot experience deserved prosperity in business despite hard work; this is also another form of barrenness.

In the Old Covenant or Testament, women who were unable to physically bear children were considered to be barren and were considered to be a curse, or the barrenness was caused by a curse. As such, barrenness was ultimately a tragedy for a married Hebrew woman. The inability to perpetuate the name of her husband and secure the orderly transfer of his estate upon his death (see Genesis 15:1-4) often resulted in insecurity and humiliation. The barren experiences isolation, alienation, rejection, depression, frustration, confusion, discouragement and disappointment.

Understanding barrenness is very important if we are to embrace this medium of processing prior to being promoted to the season of fruitfulness. It is for a reason and for a season, and not a lifetime. Understand that, like all else, barrenness has its purpose and time in our lives. It is intended to be temporary and not permanent, for a season prior to our spiritual transition. We are expected, like the children of Israel in the wilderness, to transition at the set time according to God's calendar.

Let's look at barrenness spiritually as we look at the following women of reference in the Bible who experienced physical barrenness.

If your spiritual life is not sound, healthy, or growing, this is spiritual barrenness. If such a person is not able to conceive a child, it is a combination of physical and spiritual barrenness. Hence, irrespective of the physical cause of barrenness, the root causes which supersede the physical causes are in the spiritual realm. As such, all kinds of barrenness have spiritual roots.

Barrenness can be caused by sin, curses, ungodly covenants, and the spirit of fear.

Let's look at the spirit of fear. This was the giant I had to face and fight for many years in order to break the barriers of barrenness. It was a battle I fought long and hard. Little by little, I gained ground. I feared being rejected and humiliated, being criticized and condemned, ostracized and belittled. I feared people's opinions.

When the cause of barrenness is addressed, the spiritually barren is enabled to walk into fruitfulness. They do this by acknowledging the existence of the seed already planted within and, in response, begin to get rid of all that will prevent or hinder its germination, growth, maturity, and production, ensuring its transition from being just a seed of promise being developed into being a possibility and actively a potential and reality.

The Barren Bringing Forth

There are too many spiritually barren women in Christendom who are called and chosen for such a time as this. Like Hannah, we need to travail until purpose is given birth to in the kingdom of God. At times, unknown to them, they are carrying the seed of intercession, and instead of producing accordingly, they remain barren with what the kingdom is waiting for them to give birth to so it can be populated with its kind.

They are the carriers of the seed as they bear the womb of the kingdom. Kingdom women are actually wombs called and chosen for this reason. The seed called "purpose" is implanted/conceived and needs to be incubated and nurtured to full term until birth. As such, what they carry should not be just a promise and possibility but a full-blown potential; a dream now becoming reality because the world and the kingdom are waiting on it. However, the delay is often because they fail to cooperate with God, which often results in God's will and plan being delayed or aborted or the impact limited or restricted.

When the barren becomes frustrated and travails, she gives birth to purpose in the form of their gifting and to the ministry of marriage and children, with their household and family members being saved, their spiritual life being raised to a higher dimension or level, and the connection restored to their lifetime partner or suitable help meet and support system.

The barren who become frustrated with their current condition of barrenness will travail to no avail in order to give birth to what God wants to do in the earth through whatever and whichever means He chooses. We see where Hannah, in her frustration and desperation, travailed to no avail. In response to this, Samuel, the prophet to the nation of Israel, was born. He was God's voice in the earth.

With the right mindset, the barren can certainly bring forth fruit. Yes, they can produce. They can move from being infertile and unproductive to fertile and productive and impacting and extremely influential. All things are possible with God (see Luke 1:37).

Like the barren mothers that we will be looking at, we too can and will be remembered and not forgotten when we begin to provoke heaven concerning our purpose and the destiny that has been locked up in the womb of the spirit. We can travail and give birth to it and, as such, the forgotten can be remembered. This is made possible with the right mindset.

> *And do not be conformed to this world, but be transformed by the renewing of your mind, that you may prove what is that good and acceptable and perfect will of God. (Romans 12:2 - NKJV).*

God's will cannot be fulfilled in the flesh but in and through the spirit. This begins and ends with a transformed or renewed mind, one that is governed by the spirit-man, which is fueled by the leading of the Holy Spirit and not the flesh.

In the flesh, we can never please God because the flesh always opposes the spirit-man and seeks to do his own thing, which is solely focused on pleasuring or satisfying one's selfish ego.

> *So then, those who are in the flesh cannot please God. (Romans 8:8 - NKJV).*

The barren fears being forgotten because they seem to be forsaken; however, they are never forgotten nor forsaken by God, who remembers them and causes them to be remembered.

The Barren Bringing Forth

He raises the poor out of the dust, and lifts the needy out of the ash heap, that He may seat him with princes—With the princes of His people. He grants the barren woman a home, Like a joyful mother of children. Praise the Lord. (Psalm 113:7-9 - NKJV).

According to *Isaiah 54, 1 Samuel 1-2, Genesis 15-18, 21-22, Psalm 1:3, Job 14:7-9* and John *15:1-5*, in the fullness of God's timing the barren shall come forth, spring forth, bring forth, bearing not just good and more but much fruit according to *John 15:1-5*.

As mentioned before, let us now look at these matriarchs or mothers of faith in the Bible who were considered barren. They were notable women through whom God would bring forth the promised seed or purpose; however, they had to overcome barrenness by deciding to cooperate with God.

The cooperation required is as follows:

- The first and most important step is to believe that with God, all things are possible.
- The second step is that we must become desperate to be at this place.
- The third step is to acknowledge that we have a part to play in putting an end to it.

We will also see that barrenness can be a negative generational cycle that needs to be broken. As it is in the spiritual, so it is in the natural and vice versa.

Barrenness is a faulty foundation experienced throughout the generations and needs to be fixed in order to go forward being productive.

When we look at the pattern of barrenness among the women of focus—except for Hannah—we see a negative pattern or cycle from Sarah to Rebekah to Rachel. Is this just a coincidence? What do you think?

The relative connections or relations: Sarah was the mother of Isaac, who was the husband of Rebekah; hence, Rebekah was Sarah's daughter-in-law. Rebekah was the mother of Jacob, Sarah's grandson, and Jacob was Rachel's husband. All three women here had their wombs locked or suffered barrenness. What do they have in common? A negative cycle that could have been broken and was broken. God looked upon them, took careful note of or remembered them, and favored them by opening up their womb so that all the families of the earth would be blessed through them.

For the barren to bring forth, the negative cycle and generational curse must be broken.

Also, we see that the matriarchs' barrenness highlights that God is the God of seasons and times and has the power at His disposal to change it for His good pleasure at any second, minute, or hour. He can, and will, disrupt the continuity in the transition from one generation to the other and then make His choice of the heir to continue in the covenant with His people.

God holds the key to open and close the physical and spiritual womb as seen in Genesis 25:21, Genesis 29:31, and 1 Samuel 1:6. God closed up the wombs of the women in Abimelech's household because he had taken Abraham's wife, Sarah, as seen in Genesis 20:14-18. We see in 2 Samuel 6:14-23 where King David was criticized by his wife, Milcah, for his undignified worship to God, and as such, she remained barren for the rest of her life because she dishonoured God by dishonoring the man of God. God closed up her womb, so she was now cursed with barrenness.

God is the ultimate source of fertility and conception; as such, the opening and closing of the womb is attributed to the divine destiny, even for the fertile woman, as seen in Genesis 20:17. Also, it is evident that these women experienced or suffered shame as a result of their condition of barrenness. In those days, this state of women would be attributed to either them having some hidden sin or flaw.

We see in 1 Samuel 1:5-8 where Hannah was provoked and humiliated because her womb was shut. Her rival, Penninah, saw her as a reproach. She taunted and haunted her daily and made her life a misery. Thanks be to God, we see where God further turned it around for her good and His glory. God turned her pain into purpose, her misery into ministry, her test into a testimony, and her mess into a message that even today, to many, including you and I, is a point of reference when our state of barrenness doesn't seem to make any sense at all.

Sarah was despised in Hagar's eyes, as seen in Genesis 16:4. Rachel pleaded out of frustration to Jacob (see Genesis 30:1). God remembers and takes note of the barren. I can imagine this declaration as follows was one made by all four women after they were delivered from their state of barrenness:

> *I waited patiently for the LORD; and He inclined to me, and heard my cry. He also brought me up out*

of a horrible pit, out of the miry clay, and set my feet upon a rock, and established my steps. He has put a new song in my mouth—Praise to our God; many will see it and fear, and will trust in the LORD. *Blessed is that man who makes the* LORD *his trust, and does not respect the proud, nor such as turn aside to lies. Many, o* LORD *my God, are Your wonderful works which You have done; and Your thoughts toward us cannot be recounted to You in order; if I would declare and speak of them, they are more than can be numbered. (Psalm 40:1-5 - NKJV).*

CHAPTER 2: SARAH

(See Genesis 12 - 23)

"And I will bless her and also give you a son by her; then I will bless her, and she shall be a mother of nations; kings of peoples shall be from her." Then Abraham fell on his face and laughed, and said in his heart, "Shall a child be born to a man who is one hundred years old? And shall Sarah, who is ninety years old, bear a child?" Then God said: "No, Sarah your wife shall bear you a son, and you shall call his name Isaac; I will establish My covenant with him for an everlasting covenant, and with his descendants after him. But My covenant I will establish with Isaac, whom Sarah shall bear to you at this set time next year." (Genesis 17:16-17, 19, 21 – NKJV).

And He said, "I will certainly return to you according to the time of life, and behold, Sarah your wife shall have a son." (Sarah was listening in the tent door which was behind him.) Now Abraham and Sarah were old, well advanced in age; and Sarah had passed the age of childbearing. Therefore Sarah laughed within herself, saying, "After I have grown old, shall I have pleasure, my Lord being old also?" And the

The Barren Bringing Forth

Lord said to Abraham, "Why did Sarah laugh, saying, 'Shall I surely bear a child, since I am old?' Is anything too hard for the Lord? At the appointed time I will return to you, according to the time of life, and Sarah shall have a son." (Genesis 18:10-14 – NKJV).

And the Lord visited Sarah as He had said, and the Lord did for Sarah as He had spoken. For Sarah conceived and bore Abraham a son in his old age, at the set time of which God had spoken to him. And Abraham called the name of his son who was born to him—whom Sarah bore to him—Isaac. (Genesis 21:1-3 – NKJV).

Sarah was the wife of Abraham and the mother of Isaac (the seed of promise and the covenant child). Sarah was ten years younger than her husband, who was her half-brother because they shared the same father but different mothers (see Genesis 20:12).

Although a promise was given or made that a chosen nation would be born through them, Sarah, who was barren at the time of the promise, remained barren for twenty-five long and agonizing years of disappointment, discouragement, and frustration as she became impatient. Ten years after receiving the word of promise or prophecy, out of her impatience, doubt, fear, and insecurity, she decided to help herself and God fulfill what God had said concerning her. According to the reality of her life, bearing a child seemed impossible, and the waiting period was too long. She just could not see as God saw. She could not see it becoming a reality with the evidence of nature making a statement that this is humanly impossible, as seen in Genesis 18:11-12.

As a result, she tampered with God's plan and messed it up, but not in its entirety because, as it naturally is, God is always in control. He will not allow His plan to be foiled, fouled, derailed, or aborted. When He says it, that settles it, even when it is meddled with.

Sarah's decision did not work for her but against her. The maidservant she gave to her husband to bring forth the child she thought was impossible to be birthed by her began to ridicule her upon conception. God did not need her help but just her cooperation in remaining in faith as she waited.

Yes, it is okay to say Sarah blundered, but she was not alone in it. Abraham, who God personally gave the promise to, like Adam as seen in Genesis 3:6, participated in the misfit because of doubt or unbelief, or should we call it "spouse pressure." He ran along with Sarah's suggestion and plan without questioning it or exercising his God-given authority as the head: the prophet, priest, and king. Can we safely say he somewhat had an "Ahab spirit" that just gave in to satisfy his wife's demand (see Genesis 16:1-5, 1 Kings 21:1-16)? At this point, he was not very strong or assertive, and he allowed Sarah to lead him on.

Just as it was in the beginning in the Garden of Eden, Sarah and Abraham were visited and a seed of doubt sown in their spirit, resulting in them asking the question, "Did God say?" (see Genesis 3:1, 16:1-6, 18:9-15).

God's Word cannot—and will not—return to Him void. Even though Sarah messed up, God moved heaven and earth to fulfill His plan. Heaven and earth moved into action to sanction what God had said would happen (see Genesis 12:2-3, 15:4, 17:1-8, 15-21).

As seen in Genesis 17:4-5 and Genesis 17:15-16, God sought to settle their doubts and fears by giving them a name change, which was significant to the shift or change in their times and seasons of barrenness. The drought was over, and there was now sounds of an abundance of rain. It was time to unveil, unpack, unwrap, unlock, and release. He who had the key to barrenness was now about to unlock and release fruitfulness. God said to Abraham in Genesis 17:5 that his name had been changed because he *"has been made,"* not *going to be* but *has been made* the father of many nations. At the time of that proclamation or declaration, there was no physical evidence of the manifestation, but God said it, and that settled it.

We see in Genesis 21:1-7 with Sarah, now being at the age of ninety and Abraham being one hundred years old, God fulfilled what He had already set, settled, and planned in heaven according to the full volume of the book written concerning them (see Psalm 40:7, Hebrews 10:7)—that good work which He had begun in them was accomplished as seen in Philippians 1:6. It was not accomplished and fulfilled by their might or strength or any help from them as was offered (see Genesis 18:14), but by His Spirit (see Zechariah 4:6). From her womb came the promised offspring.

God does nothing partially or halfheartedly. He did not say from Abraham only but from Abraham and Sarah; hence, the child born to Abraham through Hagar could not suffice for what God had intended. It had to be according to His plan and not that of man's or man's intervention. It was not in accordance with their estimation but God's divine ordination. With the right formulation—Abraham and Sarah—the barren did bring forth according to God's plan which was established from the foundation of creation.

CHAPTER 3: REBEKAH

(See Genesis 24 - 25)

This is the genealogy of Isaac, Abraham's son. Abraham begot Isaac. Isaac was forty years old when he took Rebekah as wife, the daughter of Bethuel the Syrian of Padan Aram, the sister of Laban the Syrian. Now Isaac pleaded with the Lord for his wife, because she was barren; and the Lord granted his plea, and Rebekah his wife conceived. But the children struggled together within her; and she said, "If all is well, why am I like this?" So she went to inquire of the Lord. And the Lord said to her: "Two nations are in your womb, Two peoples shall be separated from your body; One people shall be stronger than the other, and the older shall serve the younger." So when her days were fulfilled for her to give birth, indeed there were twins in her womb. And the first came out red. He was like a hairy garment all over; so they called his name Esau. Afterward his brother came out, and his hand took hold of Esau's heel; so his name was called Jacob. Isaac was sixty years old when she bore them. (Genesis 25:19-26 – NKJV).

Rebekah was the wife of Isaac and the mother of Esau and Jacob. Prior to his death, Abraham instructed that a suitable helpmeet or wife be sought for the promised son or his heir, Isaac (see Genesis 24:1-7). As per prophetic instructions given and followed, clarity was sought and received with confirmation, and Rebekah was given in hand to Isaac to be his lawful wedded wife. Isaac did find favor, as seen in Proverbs 18:22. Yes, they went in search of and found; however, Rebecca was not searching, and she was found. God will grant His desires for you, even when you personally do not have them. He is always thinking of you, even when you are not thinking of Him. God will place those desires of His within you, even if you did not initially have them, because they are a part of His plan concerning you. In doing so, He successfully fulfills His will in and through your life, all for His glory.

For Isaac's wife, a search ensued, and his missing rib and suitable helpmeet or support system was found. Yes, his soulmate and partner for life—his wife—was found because even before he was formed, she was ordained to be his wife. Even in barrenness, God has already fulfilled and completed what is not yet seen or experienced in the natural.

There was one glitch, however, she was barren. She was beautiful and made Isaac complete—a suitable helpmeet—but barren. This was not in Isaac's plan. He did not expect nor was he prepared for it. Rebekah was barren, but according to Genesis 25:21, when Isaac interceded on his wife's behalf, the God of heaven who has the keys to open and shut heard and answered his prayer favorably with the extraordinary (see Genesis 25:22-24).

Like her mother-in-law, Rebekah was barren. Possibly, I could say barren for a reason and for a season. As a result, she received double blessing for her humiliation and frustration. Her conception yielded her a set of twins. Through her husband's intercession, the heaven that was shut up over her womb was now opened, and she received double for her trouble: for her shame and pain there was great gain (see Genesis 25:20-26).

> *Instead of your shame you shall have double honor, and instead of confusion they shall rejoice in their portion. Therefore in their land they shall possess double; Everlasting joy shall be theirs. (Isaiah 61:7 – NKJV).*

> *Who has heard such a thing? Who has seen such things? Shall the earth be made to give birth in one day? Or shall a nation be born at once? For as soon as Zion was in labor, she gave birth to her children. (Isaiah 66:8 – NKJV).*

Like Rebekah, if you move to break the curse and intercede accordingly, you too will receive for your shame and share of pain double for all the trouble you have experienced. You too will bring forth much fruit if you faint not.

Keep going, praying and pushing, sowing and declaring. Soon, heaven will respond to earth and you will give not still but live birth to that which needs to be unearthed.

CHAPTER 4: RACHEL

(See Genesis 29-30)

When the Lord saw that Leah was unloved, He opened her womb; but Rachel was barren. So Leah conceived and bore a son, and she called his name Reuben; for she said, "The Lord has surely looked on my affliction. Now therefore, my husband will love me." Then she conceived again and bore a son, and said, "Because the Lord has heard that I am unloved, He has therefore given me this son also." And she called his name Simeon. She conceived again and bore a son, and said, "Now this time my husband will become attached to me, because I have borne him three sons." Therefore his name was called Levi. And she conceived again and bore a son, and said, "Now I will praise the Lord." Therefore she called his name Judah. Then she stopped bearing. (Genesis 29:31-35 – NKJV).

Now when Rachel saw that she bore Jacob no children, Rachel envied her sister, and said to Jacob, "Give me children, or else I die!" And Jacob's anger was aroused against Rachel, and he said, "Am I in the place of God, who has withheld from you the fruit of the womb?" So she said, "Here is my maid Bilhah; go in to her, and she will bear a child on my knees, that I also may have children by her." Then she gave him Bilhah her maid as wife, and Jacob went in to her. And Bilhah conceived and bore Jacob a son. Then Rachel said, "God has judged my case; and He has also heard my voice and given me a son." Therefore she called his name Dan. And Rachel's maid Bilhah conceived again and bore Jacob a second son. Then Rachel said, "With great wrestlings I have wrestled with my sister, and indeed I have prevailed." So she called his name Naphtali. Then God remembered Rachel, and God listened to her and opened her womb. And she conceived and bore a son, and said, "God has taken away my reproach." So she called his name Joseph, and said, "The Lord shall add to me another son." (Genesis 30:1-8, 22-24 – NKJV).

Rachel was the younger daughter of Laban and the second wife of Jacob, who was tricked into marrying the eldest first, even though he had asked for the youngest and was told he had to work for her. Rachel was the mother of Joseph.

Before giving birth to Joseph and later Benjamin, she became bitter and envied her older sister, Leah, to whom Jacob had also married. Leah had given birth to four sons, while Rachel could have none. This must have been quite burdensome and painfully humiliating. Even though she was Jacob's favourite, it wouldn't suffice for the pain of barrenness that she was feeling. Her desire was not forthcoming, and anxiety and frustration were taking a toll on her.

The Barren Bringing Forth

It must have been extremely frustrating and devastating for Rachel to stand by and watch Leah produce while she remained barren. As a result, insecurity and jealousy walked in because she became overwhelmed and felt defeated. It led her to become bitter and hateful, and, in her bitterness, she angrily demanded a child of her husband. This caused a bit of unsettledness and dysfunctionality because of the anxiety. Inconsideration developed because of her condition of barrenness as she suffered the pain of humiliation. Such a request of her from her husband was quite unreasonable because she knew that her barrenness was beyond his control.

As such, like Sarah, she offered to help alleviate the pain and stress of the discomfort and shamefulness of barrenness. She did not know that barrenness was a part of the process to fruitfulness as she had to be pruned of anger, jealousy, and bitterness prior to being made able to produce fruit after her kind. She was easily agitated because of the barrenness, and this pushed her to make unreasonable demands of her husband, who had absolutely no control over what God was in control of. God had withheld from them for some unknown reason that had not been revealed.

God knew the why, how, and when because He knew the beginning from the end, even before time began. Before Jacob and Rachel were conceived and met (see Jeremiah 1:5, 29:11, Psalm 139:1-7, 13-16), God ordained them to be a suitable support system for each other. There is no doubt that Jacob had found his missing rib, even when he was met by deceit (see Genesis 25:24-34 and Genesis 27).

Jacob was destined to be married to Rachel but, like Rebekah, barrenness again showed up in the picture, and Rachel did not see her future looking bright without a child. She was threatened by Leah's fertility, who was being extremely fruitful and was multiplying, while Rachel was merely existing as a wife but could not produce accordingly because her womb was shut.

I can imagine all the measures she may have put in place and the different means of getting it done, but to no avail. She just could not get the satisfaction of experiencing the joy of conception. Instead, all she experienced was sheer humiliation. However, in the fullness of time, just like the others, God remembered and took note of her situation in response to her intercession and enabled conception (see Genesis 3:22).

God remembered His covenant with Abraham and heard and answered Rachel's prayer. At the set time assigned to put an end to her barrenness and torture, He opened her womb, and she gave birth to two sons: Joseph and Benjamin. She too received double for her trouble and great gain for her pain.

Rachel provoked heaven in her own way when she provoked her husband to give her a child lest she die and also provoked heaven in her prayer of frustration, as seen in Genesis 30:22. He saw Rebekah's action of desperation when she gave her servant to bring forth that which she could not have done because of the physical restriction in her womb.

One key point to note here is that out of desperation comes provocation, and this audacious faith is what moves God into immediate action of favour, the suddenly, and acceleration of the divine manifestation from barrenness to fruitfulness and in abundance or excess.

As seen in all the cases of barrenness presented, character and faith was put to the test.

CHAPTER 5: HANNAH

(See 1 Samuel 1-2:1-11, 22)

Now there was a certain man of Ramathaim Zophim, of the mountains of Ephraim, and his name was Elkanah the son of Jeroham, the son of Elihu, the son of Tohu, the son of Zuph, an Ephraimite. And he had two wives: the name of one was Hannah, and the name of the other Peninnah. Peninnah had children, but Hannah had no children. But to Hannah he would give a double portion, for he loved Hannah, although the Lord had closed her womb. And her rival also provoked her severely, to make her miserable, because the Lord had closed her womb. So it was, year by year, when she went up to the house of the Lord, that she provoked her; therefore she wept and did not eat. Then they rose early in the morning and worshiped before the Lord, and returned and came to their house at Ramah. And Elkanah knew Hannah his wife, and the Lord remembered her. So it came to pass in the process of time that Hannah conceived and bore a son, and called his name Samuel, saying, "Because I have asked for him from the Lord." And she said, "O my Lord! As your soul lives, my Lord, I am the woman who stood by you here, praying to the Lord. For this child I prayed,

The Barren Bringing Forth

and the Lord has granted me my petition which I asked of Him. Therefore I also have lent him to the Lord; as long as he lives he shall be lent to the Lord." So they worshiped the Lord there. (1 Samuel 1:1-2, 5-7, 19-20, 26-28 – NKJV).

And the Lord visited Hannah, so that she conceived and bore three sons and two daughters. Meanwhile the child Samuel grew before the Lord. (1 Samuel 2:21 – NKJV).

Hannah was the wife of Elkanah. She was unable to bear children and suffered at the hands of her adversary because of this. In her desperation, she bowed, vowed and was vindicated in the presence of her enemy. Yes, her table was prepared and presented right there in the sight of her adversary, Peninnah, who jeered and mocked openly and was now standing to see Hannah being blessed in abundance, according to Psalm 23:5.

Hannah's prayer (see 1 Samuel 1:10-11) demonstrated the Godly way to handle situations you have no control over. She sought God for only what He could do (see Psalm 34:15). She rolled the stone away by interceding, and God called forth her dead situation from the tomb. Her womb was brought back to life, and she brought forth not just one but five, representing God's manifested grace and mercy who blesses the righteous and encompasses them like a shield, as seen in Psalm 5:12.

The effectual fervent prayer of the righteous avails much (see James 5:16). Hannah's repetition in referring to herself as a maidservant, as seen in 1 Samuel 1:11, 18, exhibited her humility and dependency on God. Being firm in her conviction and fully persuaded in faith, her prayers were answered.

After receiving the consolation of an answered prayer by Eli, she worshiped in thanksgiving and great expectation, and the Lord remembered her and brought fruitfulness to her once fruitless womb. God removed her reproach, shame, and social disgrace associated with her time of barrenness. He replaced it with His amazing, abundant, sufficient, efficient, abounding, unlimited, and great grace.

The Lord remembering her does not mean He had forgotten her but that her persistent intercession provoked Him to now move speedily, favorably, and suddenly to answer her and unfold His purpose by fulfilling her ordained need through this seed.

Note that she had four other children thereafter; however, the purpose was fulfilled with Samuel because, like Isaac's birth by Sarah, God's covenant was with the child of purpose.

Unknown to Hannah, the burden of her personal barrenness being experienced was similar to that which was being experienced by God concerning His nation, Israel, who was barren for a lack of revelation. As such, God permitted the birth of Samuel, prepared and then called and raised him up to fulfill this purpose as seen in 1 Samuel 3.

There was very little prophetic activity and, as such, Hannah interceded for her personal need to be met in the form of a child. Her answered prayer would also be an answered prayer for God's people. God needed to supply or fulfill that which was needed as He sought a voice through which He could speak to His people.

The Barren Bringing Forth

Giving birth to her son was also giving birth to the will, plan, purpose and blessing to the nation of Israel in the form of the prophet Samuel. When we pray for a blessing, just know that our intentions must be selfless. We should pray from the revelation that the blessing will be used to advance God's kingdom, help others and be of benefit to us or compliment us. Never intercede with a selfish motive. Whatever you desire to be birthed should first and foremost bring glory to God in advancing His kingdom and adding value to the lives of others.

As Hannah entrusted the longings or desire of her heart to God in consistent and intense intercession, He moved on her behalf and advanced His larger plan through her at the same time. For Hannah, she knew that her period of infertility would end when God blessed her womb by opening what He had shut, as seen in 1 Samuel 1:5-6.

Let's look at the story of Hannah and Sarah: two barren women who were desperate to have children. Yes, they did have that desire because God had placed it in them; He did this for a purpose. He had a plan for these children to be born of them. They were intended to show forth God's glory in the earth. They were to be a blessing, deliverer, message, ministry: they were seeds of purpose.

Hannah, in response to her desire, got out of her flesh and stayed in the spirit because she understood that it was not about her but about He who is faithful in all things. With this knowledge, she stayed in consistent, persistent and earnest prayer, birthing out what she carried within which was not yet conceived.

There was no literal seed planted in the womb and, to her knowledge and based on her natural experience, she was barren. What is important to note is that because of her faith, Hannah, unlike Sarah, in her pain of barrenness, contended in prayer for that which never physically existed, but she knew and was persuaded was alive and well in the spirit. She could only have done this because she stayed in the spirit. She was not conformed to the standard of the world but was transformed by a renewed mind. This mind, which was also in Christ, enabled her to have a different approach to a similar situation that Sarah had. Hannah's response was different because of her connection and spirituality. She walked in the flesh but did not operate in the flesh but in the spirit.

Let's look at Sarah's response in her condition or situation of barrenness. Sarah was experiencing confusion, while Hannah had clarity on that one thing she desired because she was constantly seeking the Lord in prayer about it.

Sarah, unlike Hannah, did not travail in her pain as she waited. She acted in her flesh and interrupted God's plan by seeking help through a slave woman. This worked against her, not for her. However, because God is good, great, and merciful, and because He knew the plans He had for Abraham because of His covenant with him to bless him through this channel, He overlooked and bypassed Sarah's mistake, mishap, and stupidity in order to ensure that His will and perfect plan was done. Many are man's plan but it's God's plan and purpose that will stand as stated in Proverb 19:21.

There is nothing too hard for God. God can turn things around to line up with His plan for our lives; however, we must stay in the spirit and have a renewed mind. He can turn nothing into something. He can turn what the enemy meant for evil for your good. The enemy meant the taunting of Hannah by Peninnah to have destroyed her mentally but it built her spiritually. It turned her into a lean, mean prayer machine that produced results that turned her enemy's head away in shame and made her behold the glory of God or the hand and finger of God on and in her life. Instead of none, she gave birth to five children (see 1 Samuel 2:21, Isaiah 54:1-3). Sarah had just one. Sarah's one seed, however, resulted in a nation being born, including Hannah and her family.

Hannah, after she received the answer, had a new song and a new countenance (see 1 Samuel 1:18-19, 1 Samuel 2:1-10). She was no longer ashamed or walking in disgrace because her story and season had changed: from empty to plenty, from stress to rest, from ashes to beauty, from heaviness to praise, from sadness to gladness, from mourning to dancing, from weeping to worship. God had turned it around for her. What the enemy meant for evil was turned around for her good and, ultimately, for God's glory.

As Hannah pushed in prayer, she gave birth to that which had not yet been conceived. Her persistent prayer was birthing a Samuel (a prophet to the nation of Israel) that was not yet planted as a physical seed in her physical womb, but she was giving birth to it in the spirit. As such, she could leave the place of prayer fulfilled and knowing that it was done as she received the revelation of Jeremiah 1:5: even before he was conceived, even before purpose was conceived, he/it existed, and it was already a done deal. She understood this as she prayed desperately, persistently and passionately to acquire her heart's desire.

When you have reached your breaking point, everything about you changes. Hannah had reached her breaking point, and it could be seen in the way she prayed and the statements she made (see 1 Samuel 1:10-15). She reached the point where she realized that only

The Barren Bringing Forth

God could do this thing for her. He was her only option and her only alternative.

Sarah tried to help God by offering her maid, Hagar, to her husband, Abraham, to be conceived (see Genesis 16:1–16; 17:18–26; 21:1–21). Isaac interceded for Rebekah, and God answered his prayer (see Genesis 25:21). Rachel offered her maid, Bilhah, to her husband, Jacob, to go to bed (see Genesis 30:10-13). Hannah interceded and bargained with God (see 1 Samuel 1:9-11).

The Lord was the help and health of Hannah's countenance. He brought a time of refreshing as she spent time in His presence, seeking His face, interceding, and waiting in faith.

> *And she said, "Let your maidservant find favor in your sight." So the woman went her way and ate, and her face was no longer sad. (1 Samuel 1:18 - NKJV).*

Like the Psalmist in Psalm 42, she too was feeling downcast in spirit because of her tormentor as a result of her barrenness; however, her hope was still in God, knowing that the answer and the times of refreshing were found in Him only.

Like the Psalmist, Hannah needed help to be preserved during the pain of her trial which was most tormenting, frustrating, distressing, depressing, and heart-rending. She turned to her God for her help so that health could be restored to her countenance—that is, the oil of gladness and joy for the spirit of sadness and heaviness that was stealing her praise and worship and messing with her focus on producing.

CHAPTER 6: OVERCOMING BARRENNESS

Abide in Me, and I in you. As the branch cannot bear fruit of itself, unless it abides in the vine, neither can you, unless you abide in Me. "I am the vine, you are the branches. He who abides in Me, and I in him, bears much fruit; for without Me you can do nothing. If anyone does not abide in Me, he is cast out as a branch and is withered; and they gather them and throw them into the fire, and they are burned. (John 15:4-6 - NKJV).

To overcome barrenness, there must first be a frustration that leads to desperation, which then leads us to take the necessary drastic action. We must begin to bear fruit, and this can be done first and foremost by staying connected to God; by abiding in Christ through His Word and making Him, who is the Word, our source of meditation (see Joshua 1:8 and Psalm 1:2-3).

Put your trust in God alone. Be obedient, faithful, committed and fear God and, like Abraham, walk blamelessly before God. Like David, be humble and fearless, trusting and confident in all that is required of you to bear much fruit.

Fear nothing or no one but be courageous and strong by enquiring of God each step of the way, and encouraging yourself in God every day.

To overcome barrenness, you must discover what you have been created, called, chosen, and commissioned to do. What is your purpose?

We must remove the limitations and be prepared to step out, even when we feel fearful and insecure. Leave the comfort zone of the familiar and step into the unknown (see Genesis 12:1-3). When you have overcome barrenness, others, through you, will also be and become blessed. Through Hannah breaking the barrier of barrenness through her intercession, she was able to bring forth a prophet who was a blessing to the nation of Israel. Through Abraham and Sarah breaking the barrier of barrenness, nations, including their own, were saved from a deadly famine (see Genesis 41-47).

Unlike Sarah, we must see as God sees and not what our emotions and carnal mind dictate to us. A mindset that is spiritually renewed and transformed will give good, better and the best results as needed. Total dependence or reliance on God is extremely necessary (see Proverbs 3:5-6). This mind chooses in all things to seek God's mind on things and ask His guidance in any and everything.

God doesn't need our help; all He needs is our cooperation. Like a glove, we need to be flexible and available so His hands can fit comfortably in our lives so we can be usable.

We need not be like Sarah but rather like Hannah. Wait patiently with the right mind, one that is in expectation and anticipation with prayerful supplications and the right intention for God's glorification. We will receive God's divine manifestation within His time as we do this. Just cultivate and maintain a renewed mind.

Like Hannah, do not be ashamed to approach the throne room; become vulnerable and open before Him. Remove the veil, cloak, and mask as you enter God's presence to have an audience. There is nothing that is hidden that He doesn't know about. As such, there is no need to go in pretense and with a spirit of perfection. We must descend in humility in order to ascend in divinity.

Enter in humility and a spirit of emptiness and brokenness, and release the baggage from your spirit. He wants us to pour out so He can pour in. He wants us to get out so He can get in.

Never write off the barren. Irrespective of how long it has been, it doesn't mean this is the end. It is not over until God calls it done. It cannot be called a loss when God destined a win or victory. There is hope for a tree that is cut down that at the scent of water in the means of consistent prayer and the necessary required applications, it will spring, grow, bud, blossom, bloom, and produce again.

The first step to overcoming barrenness is to first be aware and acknowledge its existence. Secondly, you must become discontent with this position or condition. Thirdly, you must begin to have positive meditation, go into intense and consistent intercession according to divine revelation given, make your prophetic declaration, follow prophetic instructions by making the relevant applications and, with joyful expectation, anticipate the desired manifestation.

Despite the length and state of your barrenness, God can do nothing less than what He has done in and through these women, including Hannah. As He has done it before, He will do it again because He is the same God then and now. He never changes, even though times and seasons change. He still remains the same—yesterday, today, and forever (see Hebrews 13:8).

As the seasons and times of these women changed at the scent of water, their barren wombs sprang into action at the sounds of an abundance of rain with the freshness or dew of heaven. God did a new thing for them; He can do the same for you if you permit Him.

The areas of barrenness may be different, but the God of heaven remains the same and has the antidote of change. He has the keys to unlock whatever area of your life that has been shut down because of barrenness.

Like these women, I am a testament of this new thing being done in me. My time and season of barrenness is over. I have, like Sarah, Rebekah, Rachel, and Hannah, turned a new page or chapter in the volume of the book written concerning me. I am now in my new season, giving birth to books. As the Word of God says, "If you hunger and thirst for righteousness [fruitfulness, productivity, abundance, plenty, overflow], you shall be filled" and "Out of your belly, shall flow rivers of living water that will quench the longing and thirsting souls" (see Matthew 5:6, John 7:38). Out of my pain of barrenness, He has made my fingers the pen of a ready writer, and out of my spirit, as His Spirit speaks to me, I am now writing and flowing, growing and producing much fruit for the healing of the nation because we are called to global impact. It wasn't like this, but it was far from this. Like these once-barren women, I experienced the negative impact of the pain of barrenness that pushed me into giving birth to my purpose. Out of my pain of barrenness, through the inspiration of the Holy Spirit, I have penned several books in the series **The Journey to Destiny.**

The Barren Bringing Forth

The question was asked in Isaiah 66:8 if it is at all possible for the barren to bring forth, and indeed the answer was given (see also Isaiah 54:1-3).

From a place of barrenness to fertility, productivity, and fruitfulness. From a place of nothing to something beautiful and good. My heart is now overflowing with good things that are reproduced in the form of writing that inspires, uplifts, and gives strength and hope.

> *My heart is overflowing with a good theme; I recite my composition concerning the King; My tongue is the pen of a ready writer. (Psalm 45:1 – NKJV).*

> *The Lord God has given Me the tongue of the learned, that I should know how to speak a word in season to him who is weary. He awakens Me morning by morning, He awakens my ear to hear as the learned. (Isaiah 50:4- NKJV).*

What is it that the Lord requires of you, but you are barren and have not yet begun to bring forth? Of all the women we have studied, you can safely use Hannah as a point of reference as to how you can break it, break free, and walk into the place of fruitfulness and into your prophetic destiny.

Stay in the place of prayer and pray accordingly. Be consistent and persistent and apply physically whatever strategy or application is needed. Even though Hannah did what was necessary spiritually, she had to apply the physical part of it by becoming intimate with her husband as she discerned the times and seasons.

The Barren Bringing Forth

It is critical to know your season so there will be no delay, denial, or need for another trial. Going around the mountains and in the wilderness in circles is not God's plan for our lives. His intent is for us to go forward and produce good and much fruit as the seasons beckons it.

Barrenness was from the beginning, not just now. But the God who put an end to it then can also do it now. The same procedure remains; it also never changes. Apply the principles shared accordingly and cooperate with God to break this negative cycle and establish a new order in your life—the order of God as established from the foundation of the earth when He created the universe.

What is rightfully yours is yours as an heir of His kingdom and a seed of Abraham. However, we must do our part to access it. Claim your inheritance, fight for it, demand it, and step out of barrenness or emptiness into fruitfulness and plenty, and be blessed. Produce and keep producing much good fruit so that nations can benefit or be blessed by it. Discover your why or purpose, walk in it, and live a life of victory, not defeat.

> *Then God blessed them, and God said to them, "Be fruitful and multiply; fill the earth and subdue it; have dominion over the fish of the sea, over the birds of the air, and over every living thing that moves on the earth." (Genesis 1:28 – NKJV).*

Like Hannah, it is time to intercede for this one thing if you are to give birth to it in the season or set time of your life. The God who changes the times and seasons is the God of the times and seasons and grants triumph and victory for every battle fought. He is turning your seasons and times. It is the time of birthing; position yourself for the crowning of that which He has deposited in you. It is the season to give birth and life to it. You have been carrying it for a long time now. It will not be aborted. There will be no stillbirth. It will be born alive. It is your season and time; you must sense the crowning and the intensity of the birth pains and keep pushing because something is happening in the realms of the spirit. There is a crowning. Purpose is emerging.

If you have been pushing, keep going; don't stop. If you have not been pushing, it is time to sense what is happening, position yourself, and begin to push as you sense the timing and contractions or dilation. The chief midwife, the Holy Spirit, is monitoring. He is our Helping Presence who gently guides and directs the birthing process.

> *I will instruct you and teach you in the way you should go; I will guide you with My eye. (Psalms 32:8 – NKJV).*

Fear not. Trust God and the process, and cooperate with Him fully during this season of your release because it is going to happen. It is happening, and you must see and believe in order to receive or experience what is coming and what God is doing. There is a shifting, turning, moving, crowning, and birthing. Obeying prophetic instructions is critical in the birthing season.

> *Do not be like the horse or like the mule, which have no understanding, which must be harnessed with bit and bridle, else they will not come near you. (Psalms 32:9 – NKJV).*

The Barren Bringing Forth

The God of seasons and times is working assiduously and effortlessly to accomplish and fulfill His promise to you, just as He did to Sarah and Abraham. All He is asking for is your cooperation with Him in the process and that you do not mess up what He is doing because of doubt, unbelief, negative confessions, declarations, and actions. Do not delay the manifestations any longer. The promise is now long overdue, and there is absolutely nothing impossible or too hard for God to do in, for, and through you. It is up to you to be ready when He is and cooperate accordingly.

Ask or enquire of God in this season, and it will be revealed or downloaded to you. It will be revealed because its purpose is not for you or about you but rather for those waiting on and relying on it. As such, you must give birth to it. No more delay; it is time. It is time to be unveiled, unpacked and unwrapped, unlocked. It is time for the showing and revealing of the hidden or secret deposited in that earthen vessel.

> *But we have this treasure in earthen vessels, that the excellence of the power may be of God and not of us. (2 Corinthians 4:7 – NKJV).*

May the God who has all authority and power to change and shift the times and seasons move on your behalf as you move in obedience to Him. May He grant you strength, victory, and triumph in every battle and area of struggle in this season of your life, in the mighty name of Jesus Christ.

Although you may seem or feel barren, a seed has been planted and has germinated. As such, sense the contraction and the crowning and begin pushing as Hannah did. Be frustrated enough to become desperate as Rebekah and Rachel were; however, never be anxious but focused, and do not be distracted by doubt, fear, insecurity, or jealousy. Just do what is required of you and God will do the rest as the process progresses, as you seek to step out of your season of barrenness into your season of fruitfulness. Do not let another season pass you by; break that cycle now, not tomorrow or next year but now because your future is now; be present in the present.

As seen in 1 Samuel 1:17-18, Eli consoled Hannah, and she arose joyfully in anticipation of the manifestation. Like Hannah, receive the word of consolation from the throne room of heaven, rise to the occasion, and walk in the divine manifestation of production of not just fruit but much good fruit. Your time of barrenness is over. Destiny and purpose are calling. Every pulse that beats in your veins says that purpose is still alive but needs to be delivered or birthed and not die.

> *I shall not die, but live, and declare the works of the LORD. (Psalm 118:17 - NKJV).*

God takes us through cycles of barrenness before He brings forth His ultimate plan for our lives. He wants to turn our barrenness into fruitfulness because we were created to produce much fruit after our kind. The state of barrenness is a process in which God does not intend for us to stay but transition from.

Rejoice, be happy, be glad, celebrate, you barren who have not yet borne any children, God is about to because He wants to. He wants to open up your womb; He wants to make the barren woman a joyful mother of children. He wants to expand you on every hand; your territories and borders, and restore divine governmental order to your life as is established in heaven and designed to be on earth. It is time to give birth.

> *So Ahab went up to eat and drink. And Elijah went up to the top of Carmel; then he bowed down on the ground, and put his face between his knees, and said to his servant, "Go up now, look toward the sea." So he went up and looked, and said, "There is nothing." And seven times he said, "Go again." Then it came to pass the seventh time, that he said, "There is a cloud, as small as a man's hand, rising out of the sea!" So he said, "Go up, say to Ahab, 'Prepare your chariot, and go down before the rain stops you.'" Now it happened in the meantime that the sky became black with clouds and wind, and there was a heavy rain. So Ahab rode away and went to Jezreel. Then the hand of the LORD came upon Elijah; and he girded up his loins and ran ahead of Ahab to the entrance of Jezreel. (1 Kings 18:42-46 – NKJV).*

In God's covenant is love, peace and mercy: the blessing. He wants us blessed and, as such, every negative cycle of barrenness must be broken in this season of your life in order for you to walk in this promise.

> *Though the mountains be shaken and the hills be removed, yet my unfailing love for you will not be shaken nor my covenant of peace be removed," says the Lord, who has compassion on you. (Isaiah 54:10 - NIV).*

The Barren Bringing Forth

The barren must make room for fruitfulness. This is done by changing your attitude to one of gratitude and expectation, anticipation and elation.

The barren must prepare for the manifestation by making prophetic moves or actions indicating an expansion for the accommodation in response to the revelation received through the prophetic declaration and instruction.

Rejoice, usher in the manifestation of what is about to happen. Make room, spread your wings in anticipation of your elevation and practice your soaring skills. Make room so you will have the capacity to contain what is about to be poured out. Do not restrain or contain; just relax and release, extend yourself, and you will be expanded. Stretch, strengthen, and lengthen, and you will be established and made immovable, unstoppable, unbreakable, irreversible, unshakable, and untouchable because no weapon formed against you will be able to prosper, and every tongue that rises against you in judgment will be in trouble (see Isaiah 54:1-3, 17).

In this level of glory, fear, doubt, unbelief, insecurity, and anxiety cannot exist or thrive but will die in the light of His Majesty.

> *"Do not be afraid; you will not be put to shame. Do not fear disgrace; you will not be humiliated. You will forget the shame of your youth and remember no more the reproach of your widowhood. (Isaiah 54:4 - NIV.)*

The Barren Bringing Forth

At this level of glory, shame, disgrace, and humiliation is not your portion. It is a part of the story found in the past but definitely not in your present or future.

You may have been briefly abandoned, but now restoration is your portion. Righteousness is your robe, and glory is your adornment and the crown of your head. The gospel of truth is your belt, and holiness is your sash.

> *"For your Maker is your husband— the Lord Almighty is his name— the Holy One of Israel is your Redeemer; he is called the God of all the earth. The Lord will call you back as if you were a wife deserted and distressed in spirit—a wife who married young, only to be rejected," says your God. "For a brief moment I abandoned you, but with deep compassion I will bring you back. In a surge of anger I hid my face from you for a moment, but with everlasting kindness I will have compassion on you," says the Lord your Redeemer. "Afflicted city, lashed by storms and not comforted, I will rebuild you with stones of turquoise, your foundations with lapis lazuli. I will make your battlements of rubies, your gates of sparkling jewels, and all your walls of precious stones. All your children will be taught by the Lord, and great will be their peace. In righteousness you will be established: Tyranny will be far from you; you will have nothing to fear. Terror will be far removed; it will not come near you." (Isaiah 54:5-8, 11-14 - NIV).*

I declare and decree that absolutely no powers of hell will be able to defeat that which God has established concerning you.

> *And I also say to you that you are Peter, and on this rock I will build My church, and the gates of Hades shall not prevail against it. And I will give you the keys of the kingdom of heaven, and whatever you bind on earth will be bound in heaven, and whatever you loose on earth will be loosed in heaven. (Matthew 16:18-19 - NKJV).*

It is time to give birth and to accelerate as God's glory descends and heaven touches earth.

THE DECLARATORY PRAYER OF FAITH

Lord, I thank You that Your Word says that we will know the truth and the truth will make us free. I ask that as I have read, absorbed, and received, that I am being transformed by the renewing of my mind to prove what is that good, acceptable, and perfect will of God for my life, which is fruitfulness and not barrenness.

I declare and decree that barrenness comes to an end in my life, and the season of fruitfulness begins, in the mighty name of Jesus Christ of Nazareth. I declare and decree that I am springing forth from barrenness. I am bringing forth much good fruit in my season; everything that is dead and lay dry and dormant is coming forth to life, in the mighty name of Jesus Christ of Nazareth. I declare that a nation can and will be born in a day as I travail as Hannah did. I will bring forth; it will come forth; I will spring forth like a phoenix from the ash. Yes, I will rise. I command everything that is being withheld to come forth, and every seed planted to spring, grow, mature, bud, and produce after its kind, in the mighty name of Jesus Christ of Nazareth.

I call forth destiny and purpose in the form of another dimension in God, ministry, marriage, children, household and family salvation, good health, long life, and wealth. I command and declare the full volume of the book written concerning me, in the mighty name of Jesus Christ of Nazareth.

I thank You that Your kingdom come and Your perfect will is being done in my life on earth as it is ordained in heaven; therefore, I will not die but live to declare Your works, and as such, absolutely no weapon formed against me will prosper because You always cause me to triumph. I declare and decree that surely Your goodness and mercy will follow me all the days of my life, and I will live to see Your goodness in the land of the living as Your purpose, plan, and will is being fulfilled in and through my life supernaturally.

I thank You that You are delivering me from all evil that will want to keep me barren and block my destiny and purpose, in the mighty name of Jesus. I declare and decree that, in the mighty name of Jesus, I am unstuck and unstoppable. I declare and decree that every negative cycle of barrenness over my life is now broken, in the mighty name of Jesus, as I move forward to walk in my inheritance of fruitfulness and plenty. I thank You for the abundance and the robe of righteousness as I put on the whole armor. I thank You that as of today, my life will be for Your honour and glory as it will be used to impact, influence, and add value to the lives of others, in the mighty name of Jesus Christ of Nazareth.

I declare and decree that as it is ordained in heaven, it is being activated now on earth. Be it unto me, oh Lord, according to Your Word that is forever settled in heaven. I know and believe that there is absolutely nothing too hard for You because You are the God of the impossible. Thank You for doing it for me—delivering, setting me free, and causing me to live a life of liberty as You did for Sarah, Rebekah, Rachel, and Hannah. Thank You for doing it for me, all for Your glory, in Jesus' name I pray with thanksgiving. Amen.

MY NOTES

ASPIRING TO INSPIRE

My heart is overflowing with a good theme; I recite my composition concerning the King; my tongue is the pen of a ready writer. (Psalm 45:1 – NKJV).

The Lord GOD has given me the tongue of the learned, that I should know how to speak a word in season to him who is weary. He awakens me morning by morning, He awakens my ear to hear as the learned. (Isaiah 50:4 – NKJV).

BLB My Quotes:

"Being productive in my place of affliction: my pain producing purpose. As a result, you are reading because I was bleeding, and I choose to make my meditation be my medication."

BLB My Quotes:

"Like an oyster hidden in the pearl of great price for which you have to dig deep in order to seek; so is your purpose hidden in your pain and is reveal at a great price called sacrifice, so that your story can become God's glory."

The Barren Bringing Forth, divinely inspired by the Holy Spirit, was written by the Author, Brendalee Bonnie, of St. Catherine Jamaica.

Like all the others in the Journey to Destiny Series, this book was revealed to me during quiet times spent with God in His Presence, where deep and secret things are revealed and instructions are given. As I seek His face and wait, He speaks, and I begin to write as I hear.

As I am challenged, strengthened, encouraged, and comforted accordingly, I aspire to inspire others who are seeking for an answer and seeking strength and direction along the Journey to Destiny.

Finding and knowing the truth is the only way to be truly made free indeed, and this truth is found in God's Word by which I am inspired to write.

I thank the God of heaven for using me to be a ready writer and to give a word to those who need it in their time of need as they seek. I understand what it is like being on the receiving end because when His Spirit speaks to me, He relieves my troubled mind. His voice indeed makes the biggest difference one can ever find. He speaks all the time, but the deep secrets are revealed in the secret place as you set quality quiet time to seek His face and wait as you receive His grace.

This book is a ray of hope to those who are hopeless and in despair because they have been barren and, in some cases, have been like this for many years. I am a living testimony that not all hope is gone because you are not the only one who has had an encounter with barrenness. All hope is not lost because of the cross and an empty grave; there is expectation for the barren as there is hope for a tree, as seen in Job 14:7-9.

> *For there is hope for a tree, if it is cut down, that it will sprout again, and that its tender shoots will not cease. Though its root may grow old in the earth, and its stump may die in the ground, yet at the scent of water it will bud and bring forth branches like a plant. (Job 14:7-9 - NKJV).*

Barrenness was never intended to be for a lifetime but for a season, and this season is for a reason. Discern when it is time for barrenness to come to an end, and push to conceive and bring forth purpose because this is your Godly heritage—to produce much good fruit according to John 15:8.

THE JOURNEY TO DESTINY SERIES

JOURNEY TO DESTINY
S E R I E S

Brendalee Bonnie was born in the parish of St. Catherine. She gave her life to the Lord at the tender age of sixteen. Her passion is singing and living for God. Later in her life, with a new mandate and call of God on her life, she realized that she has a passion to inspire people, not just from a spiritual level, but in every other aspect of life.

Brendalee's passion for God and for helping others motivated her to successfully complete the level one counseling course at WAFIF Christian College (WCC). This accomplishment was ordained by God because it allowed her to get the proper training needed to professionally and effectively develop a God-given gift nestled within her.

As the Bible states in 2 Timothy 3:15-17, it is important to be equipped and thoroughly furnished for every good work. This course also confirmed the assignment as a helper/encourager, thereby confirming the prompting and passion to share in order to heal and empower others by giving strength to the weak, inspiration to the weary, and salvation to the lost.

With the heart of a servant, her tongue has been made the pen of a ready writer, one of the learned. The message of encouragement and empowerment is thereby communicated through her writing, giving a word in season to those who need it.

As commissioned in Luke 4:18-19 and Isaiah 61:1-2, Brendalee has answered the call to help heal the brokenhearted and help them to experience true freedom through her life-changing spiritual encounter as it is shared in this book. The objective is to help as she has been helped and to help deliver and liberate as she has been delivered and liberated as the truth is revealed. Her desire is to be able to identify with others in their struggle in the respective areas that she has struggled in and be able to help them get out as she, through the help of God, got out.

In her professional career, Brendalee works as an Administrative Assistant. She thoroughly enjoys her job, the highest point of which involves interacting with people at all levels. Each challenge encourages and pushes her to improve her personality, perception of others, and people skills. Her strengths are being passionate about God and helping, encouraging, comforting, and caring for the needs of others.

www.ingramcontent.com/pod-product-compliance
Lightning Source LLC
Chambersburg PA
CBHW050706160426
43194CB00010B/2028